MW00674012

C SHELL
Quick Reference Guide

by Anatole Olczak

ASP, Inc.

1942 University Avenue #104
Berkeley California USA 94704
(510) 548-1909 • (800) 777-UNIX • (510) 649-7926 (fax)

ISBN 0-935739-23-8

NOTICE

Although the author and publisher have made every attempt to verify the accuracy of this book, the publisher and author cannot assume any liability for errors or omissions. No warranty or other guarantee can be given as to the accuracy or suitability of this documentation for a particular purpose, nor can the author or publisher be liable for any loss or damage connected with, or arising out of, the furnishing, performance, or the use of the materials in this book. All information in this publication is subject to change without notice.

OTHER PUBLICATIONS AND SERVICES

ASP offers a full line of technical reference manuals, guides, and quick reference cards for UNIX, C/C++, Internet, and other topics. They are specifically designed for the professional who needs easy-to-access reference information to increase productivity. Please call or email (**books@aspinc.com**) for more information.

> **Korn Shell User and Programming Manual**
> **UNIX Quick Reference Guide**
> **Korn Shell Quick Reference**
> **Bourne Shell Quick Reference Guide**
> **Javascript Quick Reference Guide**
> **Tcl Quick Reference Guide**
> **Quick Reference Cards for Vi, C, C++, SCCS, HTML**

CONVENTIONS

Control characters are given as **Ctl** followed by the character in boldface. For example, **Ctl-d** specifies **Control-d** and is entered by pressing the **d** key while holding down the **Control** key. **Boldface** indicates items which must be typed exactly as given, *Italics* indicate items that are to be substituted, and brackets indicate optional items.

CONTENTS

INTRODUCTION

The C shell is an interactive command and programming language that provides an interface to UNIX. As an interactive command language, it is responsible for reading and executing the commands that you enter at your terminal. As a programming language, its special commands allow you to write sophisticated programs. It also provides the ability to customize your working environment.

The C shell was developed as a replacement for the standard Bourne shell, and is found on most systems running UNIX-based systems. It provides a number of features not found in the standard Bourne shell, such as:

▲ Command aliases
▲ Enhanced directory navigation features
▲ Filename completion
▲ History substitution
▲ Job control

There are also shareware versions of C Shell-like variants, most notable Tcsh. An Internet search should get a good number of hits on this version of the C Shell.

COMMAND EXECUTION

The **prompt** variable (default % *hostname* or # *hostname* for super-users) is displayed whenever the C shell is ready to read a command.

COMMAND EXECUTION FORMAT

command1 ; *command2*	execute *command1* followed by *command2*
command &	execute *command* asynchronously in the background
command1 | *command2*	pass the standard output of *command1* to standard input of *command2*
command1 |& *command2*	pass the standard output and standard error of *command1* to standard input of *command2*
command1 && *command2*	execute *command2* if *command1* returns zero (successful) exit status
command1 || *command2*	execute *command2* if *command1* returns non-zero (unsuccessful) exit status
command \	continue *command* onto the next line
(*command*)	execute *command* in the current shell

REDIRECTING INPUT/OUTPUT

The C shell provides a number of operators that can be used to manipulate command input/output, and files. Command, filename, and variable expansion is performed on *file*.

I/O REDIRECTION OPERATORS

<*file*	redirect standard input from *file*
>*file*	redirect standard output to *file*. Create *file* if non-existent, else overwrite. If **noclobber** set, file must not exist, or an error will occur.
>!*file*	same as >*file*, except do not check if *file* exists
>&*file*	same as >*file*, except also redirect standard error
>&!*file*	same as >*file*, except redirect standard error and do not check if *file* exists
>>*file*	append standard output to *file*. Create *file* if non-existent, else overwrite. If **noclobber** set, file must not exist, or an error will occur.
>>!*file*	same as >>*file*, except do not check if *file* exists
>>&*file*	same as >>*file*, except also redirect standard error
>>&!*file*	same as >>*file*, except redirect standard error and do not check if *file* exists
<<*arg*	read from standard input until a line that is identical with *arg* or EOF is read

3

C SHELL OPTIONS

The C shell has a number of options that control execution. They can be enabled on the **csh** command line, or from within a script file (see **MISCELLANEOUS** section).

ENABLING OPTIONS

csh *–options*   invoke the C shell with *options* enabled

LIST OF OPTIONS

–b   do not interpret next command-line arguments as options (set-user-ID scripts not executed without **–b**)

–c *file* [*args*]   read commands from *file*; put *args* in **argv**

–e   exit if a command fails

–f   enable fast start; do not read **.cshrc** or **.login** files

–i   execute in interactive mode

–n   read commands without executing them

–s   read commands from standard input

–t   exit after reading and executing one command

–v   display input lines as they are read

–V   same as **–v**, except enable before reading **.cshrc** file

–x   display commands and arguments as executed

–X   same as **–x**, except enable before reading **.cshrc** file

FILENAME COMPLETION

If enabled (by setting **filec**), partial file or user names can be completed by the C shell. If a partial file name is followed by the <Escape> character, the C shell attempts to complete the file name by matching it with a filename from the current directory. If a partial file name is followed by the **CTRL-d** character, the C shell lists all the file names that match. A prompt with the incomplete file name is redisplayed. If a partial file name begins with a ~ character, the C shell attempts completion with a user name instead of a file name. Multiple or no matches cause the terminal to beep, unless **nobeep** is set. Files with certain suffixes can be excluded on multiple matches by setting **fignore**.

ALIASES

Aliases are used as shorthand for other commands, especially frequently-used ones. The first word in each command is checked against the alias list. If there is a match, the word is replaced with the text associated with the alias. Any history substitution is then done on the alias text and arguments.

ALIAS COMMANDS

alias   display a list of alias names and their values

alias *name*   display the alias value for *name*

alias *name value*   create an alias *name* and set it to *value* (*value* may contain escaped history substitution syntax)

5

HISTORY SUBSTITUTION

History substitution allows previous commands to be modified and re-executed. The **history** variable specifies the number of previous commands accessible in the current shell. The **savehist** variable specifies the number of commands to save in the ~/.history file between login sessions.

Format: *event:word:modifiers*

event	previous command from history file:	
	!*n*	command *n*
	!*-n*	*nth* last command
	!*string*	command that begins with *string*
	!?*string*	command that contains *string*
	!!	previous command
	!{...}	separate history substitution from adjacent characters
	^*x*^*y*	substitute *x* for *y* on previous command line
word	individual word from previous command (: can be omitted if word begins with ^, $, *, ¬, or %).	
	#	entire command line
	0	first word
	n	*nth* argument
	^	first argument
	$	last argument
	%	word matched by last ?*string* search
	x-y	range of words from *x* to *y*
	-y	range of words from first to *y*
	*	all arguments (no match if only one word)
	x-	range of words *x* to second to last argument

modifier controls command/word selection (multiple modifiers must be separated with a : character). If prefixed with g, then the modification is applied to all arguments.

e	return filename suffix of first argument
h	return root pathname part of first argument
p	display new command, but do not execute
q	quote substituted words to prevent further substitution
r	return filename prefix of first argument
s/x/y	substitute first occurrence of *x* for *y*
t	return tail pathname part of first argument
x	same as q, except quote words individually
&	repeat previous substitution

FILENAME SUBSTITUTION

Unquoted words containing any of the following characters are expanded to a sorted list of filenames from the current directory. The "." and "/" characters must be explicitly matched.

PATTERN-MATCHING CHARACTERS

?	match any single character
*****	match zero or more characters
[abc]	match any characters between the brackets
[x–z]	match any character or characters in the range x to z
[a–ce–g]	match any characters in the range a to c, e to g
{s1, s2, ...}	match any string in the given set
~	substitute the home directory of the invoker
~*user*	substitute the home directory of *user*

JOB CONTROL

Job control is a process manipulation feature that allows programs to be stopped and restarted, moved between the foreground and background, their processing status to be displayed, and more. When a program is run in the background, a job number and process id are returned. Jobs being executed in the background will stop and notify you if they attempt to read input from the terminal. If **notify** is set, the Bourne shell will immediately notify you of blocked jobs.

JOB CONTROL COMMANDS

bg [%*n*]	put current or stopped job *n* in the background
fg [%*n*]	move current or background job *n* into foreground
jobs	display the status of all jobs
jobs –l	display status of all jobs along with their process ids
kill [–*signal*] [%*n*	PID]	send *signal* to job *n*, current job, or specified process-ID (default **TERM**)
kill –l	list all valid signal names
notify [%*n*]	notify user when status of current job or job *n* changes
stop [%*n*]	stop current or specified job *n*
stty [–]**tostop**	allow/prevent background jobs from generating output
suspend	suspend execution of the current shell
wait	wait for all background jobs to complete
Ctl-z	stop the current job

JOB NAME FORMAT

%, %%, %+	current job
%*n*	job *n*
%–	previous job
%*string*	job whose name begins with *string*
%?*string*	job that matches part or all of *string*

QUOTING

Quotes are used when assigning values containing whitespace or special characters, to delimit variables, and to assign command output.

'...'	remove the special meaning of enclosed characters except '
"..."	remove the special meaning of enclosed characters except $, ', !, and \
\c	remove the special meaning of character c
`command	replace with the standard output of *command*

VARIABLES

Like in other high-level programming languages, variables are used by the C shell to store values. Variable names can begin with an alphabetic or underscore character, followed by one or more alphanumeric or underscore characters. Variable names that contain only digits or special characters are reserved for special variables set directly by the C shell.

VARIABLE ASSIGNMENT FORMAT

set *variable*   set *variable* **to null**

set *variable=value*   set *variable* **to** *value*

set *variable=(value1 value2 . . . valuen)*
                                            set *variable* **to** *value1* **through** *valuen*

set *variable[n]=value*   set *variable* **element** *n* **to** *value*

set *variable[n]=(value1 value2 . . . valuen)*
                                            set *variable* **element** *n* **to** *value1* **through** *valuen*

unset *variable*   **remove the definition of** *variable*

@ *variable=expression*   set *variable* **to numerical value of** *expression*

@ *variable[n]=expression*   set *variable* **element** *n* **to numerical value of** *expression*

VARIABLE SUBSTITUTION

Variable values can be accessed and manipulated using variable expansion. Basic expansion is done by preceding the variable name with the $ character.

VARIABLE EXPANSION FORMAT

Variable expansion can also be modified by appending a history substitution modifier (:e, :gh, :gr, :gt, :h, :q, :r, :t, or :x) to the variable name. If braces are used, then the modify operator must also be enclosed.

$variable, ${variable}
: value of variable

$variable[n], ${variable[n]}
: value of word n in variable

$variable[n–m], ${variable[n–m]}
: values of words n through m in variable

$variable[–m], ${variable[–m]}
: values of words 1 through m in variable

$#variable, ${#variable}, $variable[n–], ${variable[n–]}
: number of words in variable

$0
: name of file from which command input is being read

$n, ${n}
: current shell argument n (same as $argv[n])

$*
: all current shell arguments (same as $argv[*])

These may not be used with the history substitution modifiers:

$?variable, ${?variable}
: return string 1 if variable is set, else return 0

$?0
: return string 1 if current input file known, else return 0

$$
: process ID of the current shell

$<
: substitute a line from standard input

ENVIRONMENT VARIABLES

The C shell also has environment variables. They are like regular shell variables, except that environment variables are automatically exported to child processes. The values of some environment and shell variables are shared. The C shell copies the value of the environment variables **HOME** into **home**, **PATH** into **path**, **TERM** into **term**, and **USER** into **user**, and copies each back whenever the shell variables are reset.

There are a number of environment variables that allow you to customize your working environment. Some are automatically set by the shell, some have a default value if not set, while others have no value unless specifically set.

ENVIRONMENT VARIABLE ASSIGNMENT FORMAT

setenv *var*   set environment variable *var* to null

setenv *var value*   set environment variable *var* to *value*

unsetenv *variable*   remove the definition of environment *variable*

ENVIRONMENT AND PREDEFINED SHELL VARIABLES

argv   number of arguments to the shell ($1, $2, . . .)

cdpath   directory search path for **cd**, **chdir**, and **popd** when not given a full pathname or subdirectory

cwd   full pathname of the current directory

echo   display commands and arguments before execution

fignore   filename suffixes to ignore during filename completion

filec   enable filename completion. When typed at end of a command line, **Ctl-d** displays a list of all filenames that begin with the preceding string, and **Esc** replaces the preceding string with the longest extension.

hardpaths if set, links are resolved in the directory stack

histchars one or two character string; first character replaces !, second character replaces ^ in history substitutions

history   number of previous commands accessible by the current shell (default only most recent command)

home   pathname of home directory

12

ignoreeof	if set, ignore EOF (Ctl-d) from terminal
mail	list of files to check for mail. Number can be given before filename to specify mail checking interval.
nobeep	suppress bell during command completion
noclobber	if set, > redirections can only be made to new files, and >> redirections can only be made to existing files
noglob	if set, disable filename substitution
nonomatch	if set, no error is returned on non-matching filename substitution
notify	if set, user is immediately notified of completed jobs
path	list of pathnames to search for commands
prompt	string which is displayed before each command is read. A ! is replaced with current command number (default *hostname%*, or *hostname#* for super-user).
savehist	number of command entries to save in ~/.history between login sessions
shell	pathname of current shell
status	return status of last command
time	control timing of commands. Can have one or two values, where first value specifies reporting threshold in CPU seconds, and second value specifies which resource to report. Resources given by one or more:

%D	average Kbytes of unshared data space
%E	elapsed time
%F	number of page faults
%I	number of input block operations
%K	average Kbytes of unshared stack space
%M	maximum real memory used
%O	number of block output operations
%P	total CPU time
%S	CPU time used by kernel for user's process
%U	CPU time devoted to user process
%W	number of swaps
%X	average Kbytes of shared memory used

verbose	display each command after history substitution

EXPRESSIONS

Expressions can be given to the C Shell commands like @, **exit if set** and **while**. The non-file operators are similar to those in the C programming language and have the same precedence. Null or missing values are considered zero.

FILE OPERATORS

–d *file*	true if *file* is a directory
–e *file*	true if *file* exists
–f *file*	true if *file* is a regular file
–o *file*	true if *file* owned by user
–r *file*	true if *file* is readable
–w *file*	true if *file* is writable
–x *file*	true if *file* is executable
–z *file*	true if *file* is zero length

OTHER OPERATORS

(...)	grouping (used to override precedence)
~	one's complement
!	logical negation
*, /, %	multiplication, division, modulo
+, –	addition, subtraction
<<, >>	bitwise shift left, bitwise shift right
<, >, <=, >=	less than, greater than, less than or equal to, greater than or equal to
==, !=, =~, !~	equal to, not equal to, equal to pattern, not equal to pattern (used with strings)
&	bitwise AND
^	bitwise exclusive OR
|	bitwise OR
&&	logical AND
||	logical OR
=	assignment
++, – –	increment, decrement
+=, –=	add assign, subtract assign
*=, /=, %=	multiply assign, divide assign, modulo assign

CONTROL COMMANDS

foreach *var* (*word1 word2 . . . wordn*)
        commands
end

Execute commands once for each *word* setting *var* to *word*. The **break** and
continue commands can be used to terminate or continue the loop early.

---

goto *label*

Continue execution after the line with *label* (cannot be in a **while** or **for** loop).

if (*expr*) *command*

Execute a single command if *expr* returns true

---

if (*expr1*) **then**
        commands1
else if (*expr2*) **then**
        commands2
. . .
else
        commands3
endif

Execute *commands1* if *expr1* returns true, otherwise execute *commands2* if
expr2 returns true. Execute *commands3* if *expr1* and *expr2* do not return true.

---

switch (*string*)
        case *label* :   *commands*
                                breaksw
        case *label* :   *commands*
                                breaksw
        . . .
        default: *commands*
                                breaksw
endsw

Execute commands for the **case** statement whose *label* matches *string*. If no
case statement matches *string*, then the commands associated with **default** are
executed. The **breaksw** commands causes execution to resume after **endsw**.

---

while (*expr*)
        commands
end

Execute *commands* while *expr* is true. The **break** and **continue** commands can
be used to terminate or continue the loop early.

15

OTHER COMMANDS

:	null command; returns zero exit status
break	exit from current enclosing **foreach**, or **while** loop
cd *dir*	change directory to *dir*. If *dir* not specified, change directory to $**HOME**. If *dir* is a relative pathname not found in the current directory, **cdpath** is checked.
chdir [*dir*]	same as **cd**
continue	continue at start of next **foreach** or **while** loop
dirs	display the current directory list
dirs –l	display the current directory list in long format
echo *arguments*	display *arguments* terminated with a newline
echo –n *arguments*	display *arguments* without a terminating newline
eval *command*	evaluate *command* and execute the result
exec *command*	replace current process with *command*
exit	exit from current program with value of **status**
exit (*expr*)	exit from current program with value of *expr*
glob *arguments*	perform filename expansion on *arguments*
hashstat	display statistics for hashing attempts
history	display the command history list
history [–hr] *n*	display *n* previous commands from history list:

    –h   display without command numbers
    –r   display in reverse order

limit [–h] [*resource* [*limit*]]

set or display a resource limitation. If **–h** given (only by the super-user), then hard limits are used instead of the current limits. If no *limit* is given, then the current limit for *resource* is displayed. If no *resource* is given, all current limits are displayed.

resource can be one of:

cputime	maximum cpu seconds per process
filesize	largest single file allowed
datasize	maximum data size for the process
stacksize	maximum stack size for the process
coredumpsize	maximum size of core dump

limit is a number with an optional scale factor:

*n*h	*n* hours (**cputime**)
*n*k	*n* kilobytes (all except **cputime**)
*n*m	*n* megabytes (all except **cputime**), or *n* minutes (**cputime**)
mm:ss	minutes and seconds (**cputime**)

16

login	terminate a login shell, invoke **login**, and prompt for a user name
login *user*	terminate a login shell and login as *user*
login –p	same as **login**, except preserve current environment
logout	terminate a login shell
nice [*priority*] [*command*]	
	increment/decrement process priority for the current shell or *command*. The *priority* can be (default **4**):
	+*n* increment the process priority value by *n*
	–*n* decrement the process priority value by *n* (super-user only)
nohup	ignore hangups (**HUP**) in C shell scripts
nohup *command*	execute *command* with hangups (**HUP**) ignored
onintr	terminate C shell scripts on interrupt
onintr –	ignore all interrupts
onintr *label*	execute **goto** *label* on interrupt
popd	discard top entry from directory stack
popd +*n*	discard *n*th entry from directory stack
pushd	switch top two directory stack elements
pushd +*n*	switch *n*th directory stack entry and **cd** to it
pushd *dir*	move current directory to top of directory stack and **cd** to *dir*
rehash	recompute hash table
repeat *n command*	execute *command* *n* times
set	display a list of variable names and their values
shift [*var*]	shift components of *var* once to the left, discarding the first component. If no *var* specified, use **argv**.
source [**–h**] *file*	read and execute commands from *file*. If **–h** specified, read commands, but do not execute.
time	display a summary of time used by the current shell
time *command*	display a summary of time used by *command*
umask	display current value of the file creation mask
umask *mask*	set default file creation mask to octal *mask*
unhash	disable use of internal hash table
unlimit [*resource*]	remove limitations from all or the specified *resource*
unlimit –h [*resource*]	
	remove hard limits from all or the specified *resource* (super-user only)

MISCELLANEOUS

#	anything following a # to the end of the current line is treated as a comment and ignored. If the first character of a script file is #, a C shell is invoked. Otherwise a Bourne shell is invoked.
#!*interpreter*	if the first line of a script file starts with this, then the script is run by the specified interpreter. For example, #!/bin/ksh would cause a Korn shell to be invoked. C shell options flags can also be enabled here.

DEBUGGING C SHELL SCRIPTS

The C shell provides a number of options that are useful in debugging scripts: −n, −v, and −x (see **C Shell Options**). The −n option causes commands to be read without being executed and is used to check for syntax errors. The −v option causes the input to displayed as it is read. The −x option causes commands in C shell scripts to be displayed as they are executed. This is the most useful, general debugging option. For example, tscript could be run in trace mode if invoked "csh −x tscript".

FILES

~/.cshrc	read at beginning of execution by C shell
~/.history	contains previously executed commands
~/.login	read by login shell after .cshrc file
~/.logout	read by login shell at logout

18

REGULAR EXPRESSIONS

Regular expressions are used in many UNIX commands, including **awk, ed, egrep, grep, sed,** and **vi.**

c	non-special character *c*
c	special character *c*
^	beginning of line
$	end of line
.	any single character
[*abc*]	any character *a, b,* or *c*
[*a–c*]	any character in range *a* through *c*
[^*abc*]	any character except *a, b,* or *c*
[^*a–c*]	any character except characters in range *a* through *c*
n	*nth* \\(...\\) match (**grep** only)
*rexp**	zero or more occurrences of regular expression *rexp*
rexp+	one or more occurrences of regular expression *rexp*
rexp?	zero or one occurrence of regular expression *rexp*
rexp1 | *rexp2*	regular expressions *rexp1* or *rexp2*
\\(*rexp*\\)	tagged regular expression *rexp* (**grep** only)
(*rexp*)	regular expression *rexp* (**egrep** only)

MISC UNIX COMMANDS

The following commands are frequently used in C shell scripts to
filter input and output.

awk/nawk - Pattern Scanning and Processing Language

$awk [*options*] [*'program'*] [*parameters*] [*files*]
$nawk [*options*] [*'program'*] [*files*]

Description:

The **awk/nawk** command performs actions for lines in
files that match *patterns* specified in *program*. Each input
line is made up of fields separated by whitespace.

Options:

–f*file*	get *patterns* from *file* instead of *program*
–F*c*	separate fields with character *c* (default whitespace)
–v *variable=value*	assign *value* to variable (**nawk** only)
parameters	parameters have the format *variable=expression*
files	read standard input if *files* is – or no *files* are specified

Program Format:

Patterns in program can be associated with a statement to
perform if an input line matches the pattern. The format is:

> *pattern* { *statement* }

A missing pattern always matches, and a missing
statement prints the current input line.

Patterns:

BEGIN	match before first input line
END	match after last input line
pattern1, pattern2, ..., patternn	match if *pattern1, pattern2,* or *patternn* match current input line
pattern1 && pattern2	match if *pattern1* and *pattern2* match current input line

pattern1 || *pattern2*

> match if *pattern1* or *pattern2* match current input line

!*pattern* match if *pattern* does not match current input line

/*regular-expression*/

> match if *regular-expression* matches current input line

relational-expression

> match if *relational-expression* evaluates to true

Flow Control Statements:

break exit from **for** or **while** loop

continue execute next **for** or **while** loop

delete *variable*[*expression*]

> delete element *expression* from array *variable*

do *statement* **while** (*expression*)

> execute *statement* while *expression* is true

exit skip remaining input

for (*expression1*; *expression2*; *expression3*) *statement*

> execute *statement* while *expression2* is true; loop is usually initialized with *expression1* and incremented with *expression3*

for (*variable* **in** *array*) *statement*

> execute *statement*, setting *variable* to successive elements in *array*

if (*expression*) *statement1* [**else** *statement2*]

> execute *statement1* if *expression* is true, otherwise execute *statement2*

next skip rest of the input line

return[*expression*]

> return value of *expression*

system(*command*)

> execute *command* and return status

while (*expression*) *statement*

> execute *statement* while *expression* is true

C Shell Quick Reference Guide

Input/Output Statements:

close(*file*)   close *file*

getline   set **$0** to next input record (set **NF, NR, FNR**)

getline<*file*   set **$0** to next input from *file* (set **NF**)

getline *variable*   set *variable* to next input record
(set **NR, FNR**)

getline *variable*<*file*
set *variable* to next input record from *file*

command | **getline**
pipe output of *command* into **getline**

print   print current input record

print *expression*   print *expression*; multiple expressions must
be separated with a ","

print *expression*>*file*
print *expression* to *file*; multiple expressions
must be separated with a ","

printf *format expression*
print *expression* according to C-like *format*.
Multiple expressions must be separated with
a ",". Output can also be appended to *file*
using >> or piped to a command using |

printf *format expression*>*file*
print *expression* to *file* according to C-like
format. Multiple expressions must be
separated with a ",". Output can also be
appended to *file* using >> or piped to a
command using |

Functions:

atan2(*x,y*) arctangent of *x/y* in radians

cos(*expr*) cosine of *expr*

exp(*expr*) exponential of *expr*

gsub(*regular-expression, string1, string2*)
substitute *string1* for all instances of *regular-expression* in *string2*. If *string2* is not specified, use the current record **$0**.

index(*string1, string2*)
return the position of *string1* in *string2*

int(*expr*) integer value of *expr*

length(*string*) return the length of *string*

log(*expr*) natural logarithm of *expr*

match(*string, regular-expression*)
return the position in *string* where *regular-expression* occurs. If not found, return **0**. **RSTART** is set to the starting position, and **RLENGTH** is set to the length of string.

rand() random number between 0 and 1

sin(*expr*) sine of *expr* in radians

split(*string, array*)
split *string* into *array* using **$FS**

split(*string, array, fs*)
split *string* into *array* using *fs* as separator

sprintf(*format, expr*)
format *expr* according to the **printf** format

sqrt(*expr*) square root of *expr*

srand() new seed for rand (current time)

srand(*expr*) set the seed for rand to *expr*

sub(*regular-expression, string1, string2*)
substitute *string1* for the first instance of *regular-expression* in *string2*. If *string2* not specified, use the current record **$0**.

substr(*string, x*) return the suffix of *string* starting at position *x*

substr(*string, x, n*)
return *n* character substring of string starting at position *x*

function *name*(*args,...*) {*statements*}

func *name*(*args,...*) {*statements*}

name (*expr, expr, . . .*)
define a function *name*

23

Operators:

=, +=, -=, *=, /=, %=, ^=	assignment operators
?:	conditional expression
‖, &&, !	logical OR, logical AND, logical NOT
~, !~	regular expression match/do not match
<, <=, >, >=, !=, ==	relational operators
+, -	add, subtract
*, /, %	multiple, divide, modulo
+, -	unary plus, unary minus
^	exponentiation
++, --	increment, decrement

Variables:

ARGC	number of command-line arguments
ARGV	array of command-line arguments
FILENAME	current input file
FNR	record number in current input file
FS	input field separator (default blank and tab)
NF	number of fields in the current record
NR	number of current record
OFMT	output format for numbers (default %g)
OFS	output field separator (default blank)
ORS	output record separator (default newline)
RLENGTH	length of string matched by **match**()
RS	contains the input record separator (default newline)
RSTART	index of first character matched by **match**()
SUBSEP	subscript separator (default \034)
$0	current input record
$n	*nth* input field of current record

cut - Display File Fields

$cut −c*list* [*files*]
$cut −f*list* [−d*c*] [−s] [*files*]

Description:
The cut command displays fields from lines in the specified files. The fields can be of fixed or variable length.

Options:

−c*list*	display characters from the positions in *list*
−d*c*	set field delimiter to *c* (default tab)
−f*list*	display fields specified in *list*
−s	suppress lines with no delimiter characters
files	read standard input if *files* are −, or no *files* are specified
list	comma separated list of integer field numbers; integers separated with a − indicate a range

echo - Display Arguments

$/bin/echo *arguments*

Description:
The /bin/echo command displays *arguments* on standard output. Special escape characters can be used to format arguments.

Escape Characters:

\b	backspace
\c	line without ending newline
\f	formfeed
\n	newline
\r	carriage return
\t	tab
\v	vertical tab
\\	backslash
\0*x*	character whose octal value is *x*

25

egrep - Search Files for Patterns

$egrep [*options*] 'expression' [*files*]

Description:

The **egrep** command displays lines in *files* that contain the given full regular expression pattern.

Options:

–b	precede each line with the block number
–c	display only the number of lines that match
–e *–expression*	
	search for *expression* that begins with "–"
–f *file*	get expressions from *file*
–i	ignore case of letters during comparisons
–l	display file names with matching lines once
–n	display the output with line numbers
–v	display non-matching lines
files	read standard input if no *files* are specified

expr - Evaluate Expression Arguments

$expr *arguments*

Description:

The **expr** command evaluates *arguments* as an expression. Expression tokens must be separated with blanks, and special characters must be escaped. Integer arguments can be preceded by a minus sign to indicate a negative number.

Operators (listed in order of precedence):

exp1 \| *exp2*
> return *exp1* if neither null nor 0, else return *exp2*

exp1 \& *exp2*
> return *exp1* if neither null nor 0, else return 0

exp1 \<, \<=, =, !=, \>=, \> *exp2*
> return result of the integer or string comparison

exp1 +, –, *, /, % *exp2*
> return result of the arithmetic operation

exp1 : *exp2*
> return the result on the number of matched characters between *exp1* and *exp2*

26

grep - Search Files for Patterns

$grep [*options*] *'expression'* [*files*]

Description:

The **grep** command displays lines from *files* that match the given limited regular expression.

Options:

–b	precede each line with the block number
–c	display the number of matching lines
–i	ignore case of letters during comparisons
–l	display only filenames with matching lines once
–n	display the output with line numbers
–s	do not display error messages
–v	display non-matching lines only
files	read standard input if no *files* are specified

paste - Merge Lines Between Files

$paste *file1 file2* · · ·
$paste –d *list file1 file2* · · ·
$paste –s [**–d** *list*] *file1 file2* · · ·

Description:

The **paste** command merges corresponding lines from *files*. Each *file* is treated as a column or columns of a table and displayed horizontally.

Options:

–d *list*	replace tabs with characters from *list*. If this option is not specified, the newline characters for each file (except for the last file, or if **–s** is given, the last line) are replaced with tabs. The list can contain these special characters:

\n	newline
\t	tab
\0	empty string
****	backslash

–s	merge subsequent lines instead of one
files	read standard input if *file1* or *file2* is **–**

sed - Stream Editor

$sed [−n] [−e 'script' [−f file] [files]

Description:
The sed command copies *files* to standard output and edits them according to the given editing commands.

Options:

−e *script*	execute commands in *script*
−f *file*	get commands from *file*
−n	suppress default output
files	read standard input if no *files* are specified

Command Format:
[address [,address]] *commands* [*arguments*]

> execute *commands* for each input line that matches *address* or range of addresses. If *commands* is preceded by "!", input lines that do not match the address are used.

Addresses:
If no address is given, all input lines are matched. Two addresses indicate a range.

.	current line
$	last line
n	*nth* line
/regular-expression/	
	regular expression
\n	newline

Commands:
The maximum number of addresses is listed in parentheses.

(1)a\	append the following text to the output
text	
(2)b *label*	branch to the :*label* command. If *label* is empty, go to the end of the script.
(2)c\	change lines
text	
(2)d	delete lines
(2)D	delete first line of input only

(2)g	replace input lines with buffer contents
(2)G	append buffer contents to input lines
(2)h	replace buffer contents with input lines
(2)H	append input lines to buffer contents
(1)i\	insert the following text
text	
(2)l	display input lines
(2)n	display input line; read next input line
(2)N	append next input line to current line
(2)p	display input lines
(2)P	display first line of input line only
(1)q	quit
(2)r *file*	display contents of *file*
(2)s/*RE*/*s*/*flags*	substitute *s* for the regular expression *RE* that matches input lines according to *flags*. The *flags* can consist of zero or more of:

	n	substitute for just the *nth* occurrence of the regular expression *RE* (**1–512**)
	g	substitute for all occurrences of *RE*
	p	display input line if substitution was made
	w *file*	append input line to *file* if substitution made

(2)t *label*	branch to :*label* command if substitution was made. If label is empty, go to end of script.
(2)w *file*	append input line to *file*
(2)x	exchange input line with buffer contents
(2)y/*s1*/*s2*	replace characters in *s1* with characters in *s2*. The lengths of *s1* and *s2* must be equal.
(2)!*cmd*	execute command for the input lines not selected
(1) =	display current line number
(2) {	treat commands up to closing } as a group
(0)#	interpret rest of input line as comments
(0)#n	interpret rest of input line as comments and ignore

sort - Sort-Merge Files

$sort [–cmu] [–o*file*] [–y*k*] [–z*n*] [–dfiMnr] [–btc]
   [+*pos1* –*pos2*]] [*files*]

Description:
The **sort** command sorts lines from *files*.

Options:

–b	ignore leading tabs and spaces
–c	check that the input is in sorted order
–d	sort in dictionary order; only letters, digits, and white-space are significant in comparisons
–f	sort upper and lower case letters together
–i	ignore non-printable characters
–m	merge already sorted files
–M	sort as months. The first three non-blank characters are converted to upper case and compared. (implies –b)
–n	sort by numerical value; blanks, minus signs, and decimal points can also be given (implies –b)
–o*file*	send output to *file* (default standard output)
–r	reverse the sorting order
–t*c*	set the field separator to *c*
–u	display only one occurrence of duplicate lines
–y[*k*]	use *k* kilobytes of memory to sort (default max)
–z*n*	use *n* bytes of buffer for long lines
files	read standard input if *files* is – or no files given
+*pos1* [–*pos2*]	

sort from *pos1* to *pos2*. If *pos2* is not specified, sort from *pos1* to the end of line. The format for pos1 and pos2 is:
m[.*n*] [**bdfinr**]

m	*m* fields from start of line (default **0**)
n	*n* characters from start of field (default **0**)
bdfinr	option applies to the specified key only

tr - Translate Characters

$tr [−cds] [*string1*] [*string2*]

Description:

The **tr** command copies standard input to output and translates characters from *string1* to characters in *string2*.

Options:

−c	translate characters not in *string1*
−d	delete characters in *string1* from input
−s	truncate repeated characters from *string2*

Strings:

[*a–z*]	specifies a range of characters from *a* to *z*
[*c*n*]	specifies *n* repetitions of *c*. If the first digit in *n* is **0**, *n* interpreted as octal. (default decimal)

uniq - Report Duplicate Lines

$uniq [−udc [+*n*] [−*n*]] [*file1* [*file2*]]

Description:

The **uniq** command removes duplicate adjacent lines from *file1* and places the output in *file2*.

Options:

−c	display a count of duplicate lines also
−d	display only duplicate lines once
−u	display only unique lines from the original file
−*n*	skip first *n* fields from start of line
+*n*	skip first *n* characters from the start of field

wc - Count Characters, Lines and Words

$wc [−clw] [*files*]

Description:

The **wc** command counts the characters, lines, or words in the specified files. A total count for all files is kept.

Options:

−c	display number of characters (default all options)
−l	display number of lines
−w	display number of words
files	read standard input if no *files* are specified

EXAMPLE COMMANDS

```
# Execute multiple commands on one line
      % pwd ; ls tmp ; echo "Hello world"
```

```
# Run the find command in the background
      % find . -name tmp.out -print &
```

```
# Connect the output of who to grep
      % who | grep fred
```

```
# Talk to fred if he is logged on
      % ( who | grep fred ) && talk fred
```

```
# Send ls output to ls.out
      % ls > ls.out
```

```
# Send find standard output and standard error to find.out
      % find / -atime +90 -print >& find.out
```

```
# Append output of ls to ls.out; do not check if ls.out exists
      % ls >>! ls.out
```

```
# Send invite.txt to dick, jane, and spot
      % mail dick jane spot < invite.txt
```

```
# List file names that begin with z
      % ls z*
```

```
# List two, three, and four character file names
      % ls {??, ???, ????}
```

```
# List file names that begin with a, b, or c
      % ls [a-c]*
```

```
# List the files in sam's home directory
      % ls ~sam
```

```
# Create an alias for the ls –lR command
      % alias lsl "ls -lR"
```

```
# Reexecute last command
      % !!
```

```
# Reexecute the last more command
      % !more
```

```
# Reexecute the last command, changing adm to sys
      % ^sys^adm
```

```
# Reexecute last find command, changing tmp to core
      % !find:*:s/tmp/core
```

Set **NU** to the number of users that are logged on
```
% set NU=`who | wc -l`
```
Set **TOTAL** to the sum of **4 + 3**
```
% @ TOTAL=4 + 3
```
Set **LBIN** to **/usr/lbin**
```
% set LBIN=/usr/lbin
```
Unset variable **LBIN**
```
% unset LBIN
```
Add **/usr/lbin** to the **path** variable
```
% set path=($path /usr/lbin)
```
Disable filename substitution
```
% set noglob
```
Display **$HOME set to /home/anatole**
```
% echo '$HOME set to' $HOME
```
Display the number of positional parameters
```
% echo "There are $#argv positional
parameters"
```
Display the value of positional parameter 2
```
% echo $argv[2]
```
Display the number of words in **path**
```
% echo $#path
```
Bring background job 3 into the foreground
```
% fg %3
```
Stop the **find** job
```
% stop %find
```
Display all information about current jobs
```
% jobs -l
```
Terminate job 5
```
% kill %5
```
Increment variable **X**
```
% @ X=X++
```
Set variable **X** to **20** modulo **5**
```
% @ X=20 % 5
```
Set diagnostic mode
```
% csh -x
```
Run the **dbscript** in **noexec** mode
```
% csh -n dbscript
```

\# Display the current directory stack
```
% dirs
```

\# Put **/usr/spool/uucppublic** on the directory stack and **cd** to it
```
% pushd /usr/spool/uucppublic
```

\# Check for new mail every 2 minutes
```
% set mail=(120 ~/newmail)
```

\# Set prompt to the command number and current directory
```
% set prompt=!`pwd`
```

\# Check if **VAR** is set to null
```
% if ($?VAR) echo "VAR set ok"
```

\# Check if **VAR** is set to **ABC**
```
% if ($VAR == "ABC" ) echo "VAR set to ABC"
```

\# Check if **xfile** is empty
```
% if (-z xfile ) echo "xfile is empty"
```

\# Check if **tmp** is a directory
```
% if ( -d tmp ) echo "tmp is a directory"
```

\# Check if **file** is readable and writable
```
% if (-r file && -w file ) echo "file ok"
```

\# Set a trap to ignore interrupts
```
% onintr -
```

\# Set the file size creation limit to 10 Mbytes
```
% limit filesize 10m
```

\# Remove the limitation on the **cputime** resource
```
% unlimit cputime
```

\# Read and execute the commands in **.runlog**
```
% source .runlog
```

\# Disable core dumps
```
% limit coredumpsize 0m
```

\# Display the last 10 commands
```
% history -r 10
```

\# Add group write permission to the file creation mask
```
% umask 013
```

\# Display the first and third fields from **file**
```
% awk '{print $1, $3}' file
```

\# Display the first seven characters of each line in **tfile**
```
% cut -c1-7 tfile
```

Display the first and third fields from the **/etc/passwd** file
```
% cut -f1,3 -d":" /etc/passwd
```

Display lines in **names** that begin with **A**, **B**, **C**, or **Z**
```
% egrep '[A-C,Z]*' names
```

Display lines from **dict** that contain four character words
```
% egrep '....' dict
```

Display password entries for users with the Korn shell
```
% grep ":/bin/ksh$' /etc/passwd
```

Display number of lines in **ufile** that contain **unix**; ignore case
```
% grep -c 'unix' ufile
```

Display the lengths of field 1 from **file**
```
% nawk '{TMP=length($1); print $TMP}' file
```

Display the first ten lines of **tfile**
```
% nawk '{for (i=1; i<10; i++) printf
"%s\n", \ getline}' tfile
```

List the contents of the current directory in three columns
```
% ls | paste d" " - - -
```

Display file with all occurrences of **The** substituted with **A**
```
% sed 's/The/A/g' file
```

Display your user name only
```
% id | sed 's/).*//' | sed 's/.*(//'
```

Display **file** with lines that contain **unix** deleted
```
% sed '/unix/d' file
```

Display the first 50 lines of **file**
```
% sed 50q file
```

Sort the **/etc/passwd** file by group id
```
% sort -t":" -n +3 -4 /etc/passwd
```

Translate lower case letters in **file** to upper case
```
% cat file | tr a-z A-Z
```

Display adjacent duplicate lines in **file**
```
% uniq -d file
```

Display the numbers of characters and words in **file**
```
% wc -l file
```

Display the number of **.c** files in the current directory
```
% ls *.c | wc -l
```

EXAMPLE C SHELL SCRIPTS

Here is an interactive C Shell version of the **uucp** command.

```
#!/bin/csh -f
#
#    cuucp - C Shell interactive UUCP
#
#    Anatole Olczak - ASP, Inc

# Set interrupt
onintr quit

# Get pubdir from environment, or set to default
if (${?pubdir}) set pubdir=/usr/spool/uucpublic

# Set uucp Systems file, depending on UUCP version
if (-e /usr/lib/uucp/Systems) then
    set uufile=/usr/lib/uucp/Systems
else if (-e /usr/lib/uucp//L.sys) then
    set uufile=/usr/lib/uucp/L.sys
else if (-e /etc/uucp/L.sys) then
    set uufile=/etc/uucp/L.sys
endif

# No uucp, or unknown version
if (!(${?uufile})) then
    echo "No UUCP Systems file\!"
    goto quit
endif

# Prompt for source file name
echo -n "Enter source file: "
set source=$<
```

```
# Make sure source file exists
if (!(-e ${source})) then
    echo "${source}: non-existent or not
           accessible"
    goto quit
endif

# Prompt for remote system name
echo -n "Enter remote systemname: "
set remote=$<

# Check if remote system name is valid
set ifexists=`grep ^${remote} ${uufile}`
if (!(${?ifexists})) then
    echo "${remote}: invalid system name"
    goto quit
endif

# Start the uucopy
echo "Copying ${source} to ${remote}\!${pubdir}/
${source}"
uucp ${source} ${remote}\!${pubdir}/${source}

# Exit with successful exit status
exit 0

# Exit with unsuccessful exit status
quit:exit 1
```

Here is the C Shell version of the UNIX **dirname** command.
It returns a pathname minus the last directory.

```
#!/bin/csh -f
#
#        cdirname - C Shell dirname
#
#        Anatole Olczak - ASP, Inc
#

# Check arguments
if (($#argv>1)) then
     echo "Usage: $0 string"
     exit 1
endif

# Set variables
set base=$argv[1]

# Display output
echo $base:h
```

This C Shell command returns the last part of a pathname.

```
#!/bin/csh -f
#
#       cbasename - C Shell basename
#
#       Anatole Olczak - ASP, Inc
#

# Check arguments
if (($#argv<1) || ($#argv>2)) then
    echo "Usage: $0 string [suffix]"
    exit 1
endif

# Set variables
set delsuffix
set base=$argv[1]

if (($#argv>1)) then
    set suffix=$argv[2]
    set delsuffix=yes
endif

# Display output
if (($delsuffix != yes)) then
    echo $base:t
else
    echo $base:t | sed -e 's/'$suffix'$//'
endif
```

The ccal script implements a menu-driven calendar program.
It supports addition, deletion, modification, and listing of
calendar entries. It also provides the ability to find the calendar
entry for the current day and list all calendar entries.

```csh
#!/bin/csh -f
#
#       ccal - C Shell calendar program
#
#       Anatole Olczak - ASP, Inc
#

# Set commands; use environment setting or
default
if (!(${?clear})) set clear=/bin/clear
if (!(${?editor})) set editor=/bin/vi

# Use environment variable setting or default
if (!(${?calfile})) set calfile=$HOME/.calfile

# Set filenames
set deletefile=/tmp/.delete$$
set changefile=/tmp/.change$$
set foundfile=/tmp/.found$$

# Set variables
set prompt="Press <Return> to continue"
set operation

# Set interrupt
onintr quit

# Check arguments
if (($#argv>0)) then
    echo "Usage: $0"
    exit 1
endif
```

```
# Display menu
display:
     set calfile=$HOME/.calfile
     $clear

     while (1)
          echo "     *** CALENDAR PROGRAM *** "
          echo ""
          echo " 1) Add calendar entry"
          echo " 2) Delete calendar entry"
          echo " 3) Change calendar entry"
          echo " 4) Find calendar entry"
          echo " 5) List all calendar entries"
          echo " 6) List todays calendar entry"
          echo " 7) Exit"
          echo ""
          echo -n "Enter selection or <Return> for
default menu: "
          set i=$<

          # Parse selection
          switch($i)

               case 1:
                    set operation=add
                    goto checkdate
                    goto addentry
               case 2:
                    set operation=del
                    goto checkdate
                    goto delentry
               case 3:
                    set operation=change
                    goto checkdate
                    goto changeentry
```

41

```
                        case 4:
                                set operation=find
                                goto checkdate
                                goto findentry
                        case 5:
                                goto formatentry
                        case 6:
                                set date=`date +%m%d%y`
                                goto findentry
                        case 7:
                                goto quit
                        default:
                                $clear
                                echo "Invalid selection"
                                echo -n "$prompt"
                                set tmp=$<
                                $clear
                                goto display
                endsw
        end

# Check date
checkdate:
        $clear
        echo -n "Enter date in mmdd[yy] format
(default today): "
        set date=$<

        # Verify date format
        switch ($date)

                # Default - use todays date
                case "":
                        set date=`date +%m%d%y`
                        breaksw
```

```
# Check given date
case [0-9]*:
    set length=`echo $date | wc -c | sed -e 's/^    //p'`

    # Make sure entire format is ok
    switch ($length)
        case 5:
            set mo=`echo $date | cut -c1,2`
            set da=`echo $date | cut -c3,4`
            set yr=`date +%y`
            set date=$mo$da$yr
            breaksw
        case 7:
            set mo=`echo $date | cut -c1,2`
            set da=`echo $date | cut -c3,4`
            set yr=`echo $date | cut -c5,6`
            set date=$mo$da$yr
            breaksw
        default:
            $clear
            echo "$date: invalid format - try again"
            echo -n "$prompt"
            set tmp=$<
            goto checkdate
    endsw

    # Now check individual value for day
    if (($da < 1) || ($da > 31)) then
        $clear
        echo "${da}: invalid day format - try again"
        echo -n "$prompt"
        set tmp=$<
        goto checkdate
    endif
```

43

```
                # Now check individual value for month
                if (($mo < 1) || ($mo > 12)) then
                    $clear
                    echo "${mo}: invalid month format - try again"
                    echo -n "$prompt"
                    set tmp=$<
                    goto checkdate
                endif
                breaksw


        # Invalid date given
        default:
            $clear
            echo "$date: invalid format - try again"
            echo -n "$prompt"
            set tmp=$<
            goto checkdate
    endsw

    # Proceed to the correct operation
    switch ($operation)
        case add:
            goto addentry
        case del:
            goto delentry
        case change:
            goto changeentry
        case find:
            goto findentry
        default:
            goto display
    endsw
```

```
# Display output
formatentry:
    $clear

    # Check if calendar file exists first
    if (!(-z $calfile)) then
        ( awk 'BEGIN {FS=","} \
        { print "*************************" } \
        { print "*                       *" } \
        { for (i=1; i<=NF; i++) \
        if (i==1) \
        printf "                       *\r*
DATE: %s\n", $i \
        else \
        printf "                       *\r*
%s\n", $i } \
        { print "*                       *" } \
        END { print "*************************"
}' $calfile ) | more

    # No calendar file, so go back to the top
    else
        echo "No entries found"
        echo -n "$prompt"
        set tmp=$<
        goto display
    endif

    # Prompt to continue
    echo -n "$prompt"
    set tmp=$<

    # Go to display menu function
    goto display
```

45

```
# Find specific entry
findentry:
    $clear

    # Find entry and put it in temp file
    grep "^$date" $calfile >$foundfile

    # Reset calfile to temp file and format output
    set calfile=$foundfile
    goto formatentry


# Create new entry
addentry:
    $clear
    set entry=$date

    # Make sure entry does not already exist
    set count=`grep -c "^$date" $calfile`

    # If entry exists, then prompt to change entry
    if (($count > 0)) then
        goto changeentry
    endif

    # Prompt for entry input
    echo "Enter info for ${date}: (enter <Return>
by itself when finished)"
```

```
      while (1)
            echo -n "=>"
            set line=$<

            if (("$line" != "")) then
                  set entry="${entry},${line}"
            else
                  break
            endif
      end

      # Append entry to calfile
      echo $entry>>$calfile

      # Resort calendar file
      sort -o $calfile $calfile

      goto display

# Delete entry
delentry:
      set reply="yes"
      $clear

      # Make sure requested entry exists
      grep "^$date" $calfile >$foundfile

      if ((-z $foundfile)) then
          $clear
          echo "Entry for <$date> not found"
          echo -n "$prompt"
          set tmp=$<
          goto display
      endif
```

47

```
# Double check before deleting
while (($reply != ""))

    echo -n "Delete entry for <$date>?"
    set reply=$<

    # Parse answer
    switch ($reply)
        case [yY]* :
            break
        case [nN]* :
            goto display
        case "" :
            break
        default :
            breaksw
    endsw
end

# Put all entries, except deleted in temp file
grep -v "^$date" $calfile > $deletefile

# Move temp file to calfile
cat $deletefile > $calfile

# Clean up temp files
rm -rf $deletefile $foundfile

goto display
```

```
# Change entry
changeentry:
    set reply="yes"

    # Make sure requested entry exists;
    # change field separator, commas, to
newlines
    grep "^$date" $calfile | tr ','
'\012'>$foundfile

    if ((-z $foundfile)) then
        $clear
        echo "Entry for <$date> not found"
        echo -n "$prompt"
        set tmp=$<
        goto display
    endif

    # Double check before making change
    while (($reply != ""))

        echo -n "Change/Add entry for <$date>?"
        set reply=$<

        # Parse answer
        switch ($reply)
            case [yY]* :
                break
            case [nN]* :
                goto display
            case "" :
                break
            default :
                breaksw
        endsw
    end
```

```
    # Edit requested entry
    $editor $foundfile


    # Put all entries, except deleted in temp file
    grep -v "^$date" $calfile >$changefile
    # Append changed entry to temp file in correct
    # format; change newlines to comma separators
    ( cat $foundfile | tr '\012' ',' ; echo "" )
>>$changefile


    # Move temp file to calfile
    cat $changefile > $calfile


    # Resort calfile
    sort -o $calfile $calfile


    # Clean up temp files
    rm -rf $changefile $foundfile $deletefile


    goto display

# Clean up files on interrupt
quit:
    rm -rf $changefile $foundfile $deletefile
```

DOWNLOADABLE SCRIPTS AND TIPS

Selected examples of code from ASP publications are available for free downloading from the ASP website. Now you can study and customize these programs without tedious keyboarding.

To take advantage of this special ASP customer service, visit <www.aspinc.com> and click on the "Downloads" icon. After entering basic registration information (name, street and email addresses, and phone number), you will be taken to the Download Requests page where you may choose examples from a variety of ASP publications.

QUICK REFERENCE PUBLICATIONS FROM ASP

UNIX Quick Reference Guide

You don't need to fumble through oversized volumes for quick reference lookups. Get a concise reference guide to UNIX in a single, compact handbook. The **UNIX Quick Reference Guide** contains the user and many admin commands for UNIX, including Solaris and BSD, plus hundreds of examples.

Korn Shell Quick Reference Guide

The Korn Shell is an interactive command and programming language that provides an interface to UNIX and other systems. The **Korn Shell Quick Reference Guide** covers all aspects of the Korn Shell, with complete Korn shell scripts and many examples included.

Bourne Shell Quick Reference Guide

The Bourne Shell was the original shell for UNIX, and it still remains the most widely used and distributed. The **Bourne Shell Quick Reference Guide** summarizes this scripting language and includes complete sample programs and examples. Many UNIX commands used in Bourne Shell scripting are also included.

JavaScript Quick Reference Guide

JavaScript is a cross-platform, object-based scripting language for client and server applications. The **JavaScript Quick Reference Guide** covers this scripting language and includes complete sample programs and practical examples.

Tcl Quick Reference Guide

The **Tcl Quick Reference Guide** covers the Tool control language and includes complete sample programs and practical examples.

Quick Reference Cards

Vi Reference Card
Multi-fold card summarizes commands & options of the Vi editor.

C Reference Card
Multi-fold card summarizes the C programming language.

C++ Reference Card
Multi-fold card summarizes the C++ programming language.

SCCS Reference Card
Multi-fold card summarizes the SCCS utilities of UNIX.

HTML Reference Card
Multi-fold card summarizes the 4.0 specification of HTML.

For order information, email books@aspinc.com